WITHDRAWN FROM
COLLECTION

What Is a VERB?

by Jennifer Fandel

Consulting Editor: Gail Saunders-Smith, PhD

PARTS OF SPEECH

CAPSTONE PRESS
a capstone imprint

Pebble Plus is published by Capstone Press,
1710 Roe Crest Drive, North Mankato, Minnesota 56003.
www.capstonepub.com

Copyright © 2013 by Capstone Press, a Capstone imprint. All rights reserved. No part of this publication may be reproduced in whole or in part, or stored in a retrieval system, or transmitted in any form or by any means, electronic, mechanical, photocopying, recording, or otherwise, without written permission of the publisher.

Library of Congress Cataloging-in-Publication Data
Cataloging-in-publication information is on file with the Library of Congress.
ISBN 978-1-62065-128-5 (library binding)
ISBN 978-1-4765-1737-7 (eBook PDF)

Editorial Credits
Jill Kalz, editor; Heidi Thompson, designer; Marcie Spence, media researcher; Laura Manthe, production specialist

Photo Credits
Shutterstock: Anan Kaewkhammul, 17, Bruce MacQueen, 13 (top left), dogboxstudio, 11, Felix Mizioznikov, 7, Gelpi, cover (girl), ifong, cover (feathers), Juriah Mosin, 13 (bottom left), Khoroshunova Olga, 9, Matt Jeppson, 13 (top right), Monkey Business Images, 13 (bottom right), NinaMalyna, 5, Raisman, cover (car), Rob Marmion, 21, SVLuma, 15, Viorel Sima, cover (dog), wavebreakmedia ltd, 19

Note to Parents and Teachers

The Parts of Speech set supports English language arts standards related to grammar. This book describes and illustrates verbs. The images support early readers in understanding the text. The repetition of words and phrases helps early readers learn new words. This book also introduces early readers to subject-specific vocabulary words, which are defined in the Glossary section. Early readers may need assistance to read some words and to use the Table of Contents, Glossary, Read More, Internet Sites, and Index sections of the book.

Printed in the United States of America in North Mankato, Minnesota.
092012   006933CGS13

Table of Contents

Finding Verbs 4
Show and Tell 8
Verbs Change 12

Glossary 22
Read More 23
Internet Sites 23
Index 24

Finding Verbs

A verb is one part of speech. It shows what people and things do or what they are. Every sentence has a verb.

Subjects and verbs are friends. A subject is whom or what a sentence is about. Find the subject, and you'll find the verb beside it.

Boys smile.
subject verb

Show and Tell

Action verbs show

what a subject does.

Does it crawl? Or float?

Does it bark or sneeze?

The panda eats.

Being verbs don't show action. They tell. They tie a subject to how it looks, feels, tastes, smells, or sounds.

The puppy <u>is</u> sleepy.

The blankets <u>are</u> soft.

Verbs Change

The number of subjects may change a verb's ending. Sometimes the number of subjects changes the whole verb!

One snake curls.

Two snakes curl.

The girl is happy.

The kids are happy.

Time often changes verbs. The past usually adds "ed" to the end. The future adds the word "will" in front. Most verbs follow these rules.

present: Now the car <u>zooms</u> by.

past: Yesterday the car <u>zoomed</u> by.

future: Tomorrow it <u>will zoom</u> by.

Some verbs don't follow the rules. They're called irregular verbs. Hundreds of irregular verbs are found in the English language.

present: Today the birds <u>sit</u> and <u>sing</u>.

past: Yesterday the birds <u>sat</u> and <u>sang</u>.

Some irregular verbs change letters from present to past. Others stay exactly the same.

present: Now we <u>cut</u> the vegetables.

past: Last night we <u>cut</u> the vegetables.

Nothing happens without a verb. No one *hides* or *hops*. Nothing *swims* or *floats*. Nothing *is*. A verb makes a thought complete.

Glossary

future—a time after now

irregular—not going by a rule or common method

past—a time before now

present—now

subject—a word or group of words in a sentence that tells whom or what the sentence is about

Read More

Dahl, Michael. *If You Were a Verb.* Word Fun. Minneapolis: Picture Window Books, 2006.

Ganeri, Anita. *Action Words: Verbs.* Getting to Grips with Grammar. Chicago: Heinemann Library, 2012.

Walton, Rick. *Bullfrog Pops!: An Adventure in Verbs and Direct Objects.* Layton, Utah: Gibbs Smith, 2011.

Internet Sites

FactHound offers a safe, fun way to find Internet sites related to this book. All of the sites on FactHound have been researched by our staff.

Here's all you do:

Visit www.facthound.com

Type in this code: 9781620651285

Check out projects, games and lots more at www.capstonekids.com

Index

finding verbs, 6
future tense, 14
past tense, 14, 18
present tense, 18
sentences, 4, 6, 20
subjects, 6, 8, 10, 12

types of verbs
   action, 8
   being, 10
   irregular, 16, 18
verb endings, 12, 14

Word Count: 184
Grade: 1
Early-Intervention Level: 23